From the Shoreline

Steffi Tad-y

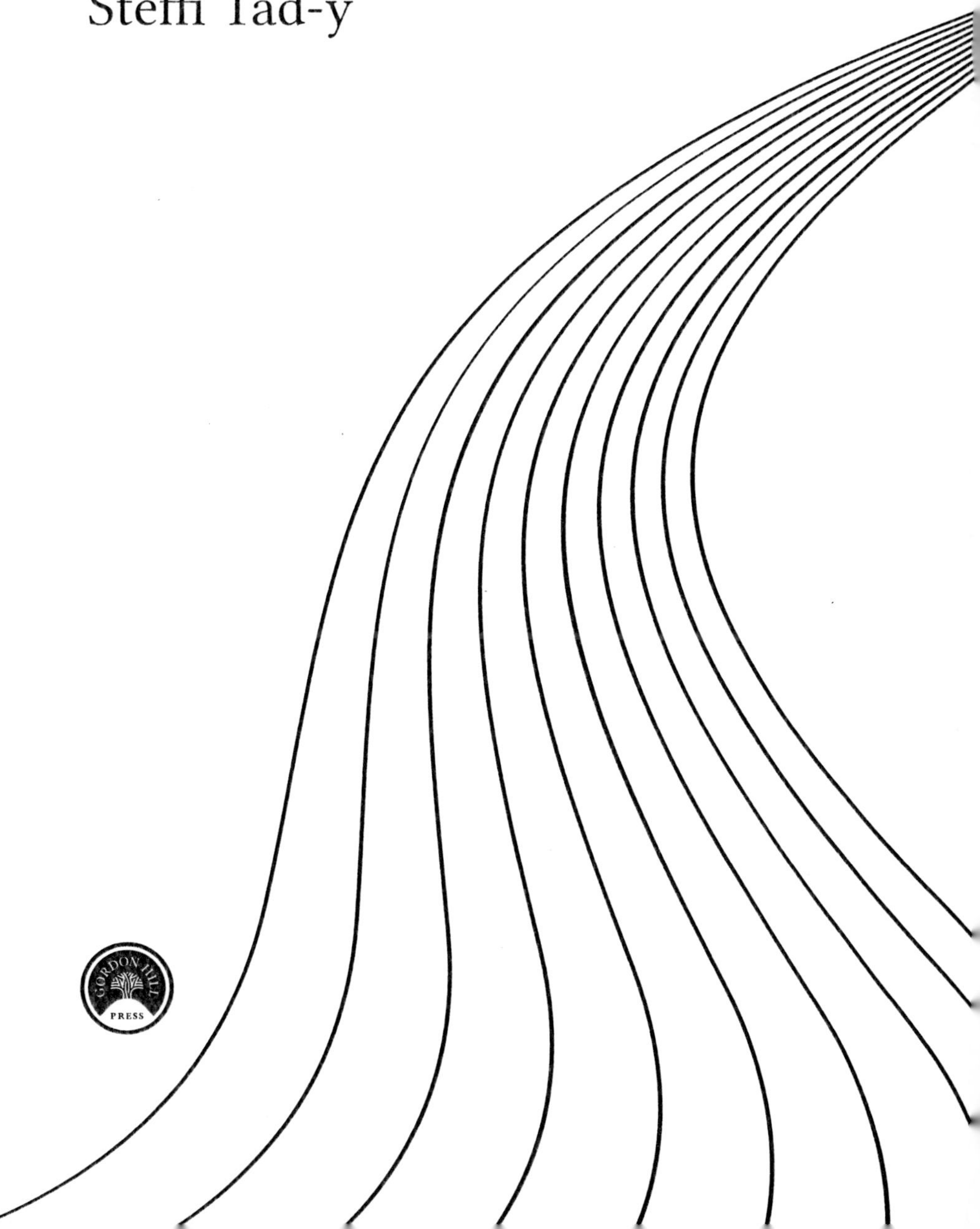

Edited by Shane Neilson
Cover and book design by Jeremy Luke Hill
Proofreading by Carol Dilworth
Set in Linux Libertine
Printed on Mohawk Via Felt
Printed and bound by Arkay Design & Print

LIBRARY AND ARCHIVES CANADA CATALOGUING IN PUBLICATION

Title: From the shoreline / Steffi Tad-y.
Names: Tad-y, Steffi, author.
Description: Poems.
Identifiers: Canadiana (print) 2021039353X | Canadiana (ebook) 20210393572 | ISBN 9781774220528 (softcover) | ISBN 9781774220634 (HTML) | ISBN 9781774220535 (PDF)
Classification: LCC PS8639.A245 F76 2022 | DDC C811/.6—dc23

Gordon Hill Press gratefully acknowledges the support of the Ontario Arts Council.

Gordon Hill Press respectfully acknowledges the ancestral homelands of the Attawandaron, Anishinaabe, Haudenosaunee, and Métis Peoples, and recognizes that we are situated on Treaty 3 territory, the traditional territory of Mississaugas of the Credit First Nation.

Gordon Hill Press also recognizes and supports the diverse persons who make up its community, regardless of race, age, culture, ability, ethnicity, nationality, gender identity and expression, sexual orientation, marital status, religious affiliation, and socioeconomic status.

Gordon Hill Press
130 Dublin Street North
Guelph, Ontario, Canada
N1H 4N4
www.gordonhillpress.com

For Al

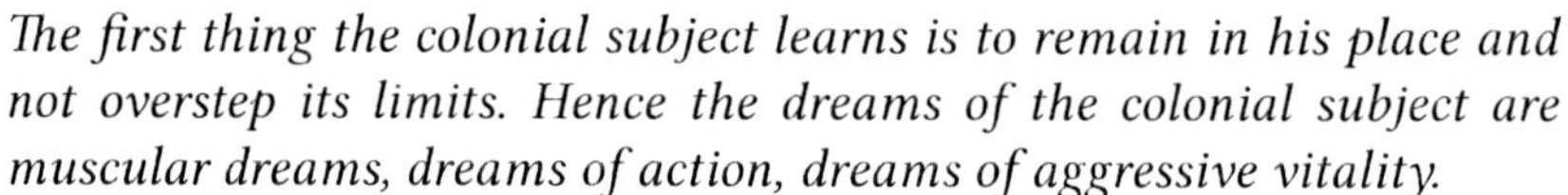

The first thing the colonial subject learns is to remain in his place and not overstep its limits. Hence the dreams of the colonial subject are muscular dreams, dreams of action, dreams of aggressive vitality.

— Frantz Fanon

You are always whole. Except when you're dreaming. You are a quarter open.

— Aracelis Girmay

Table of Contents

I

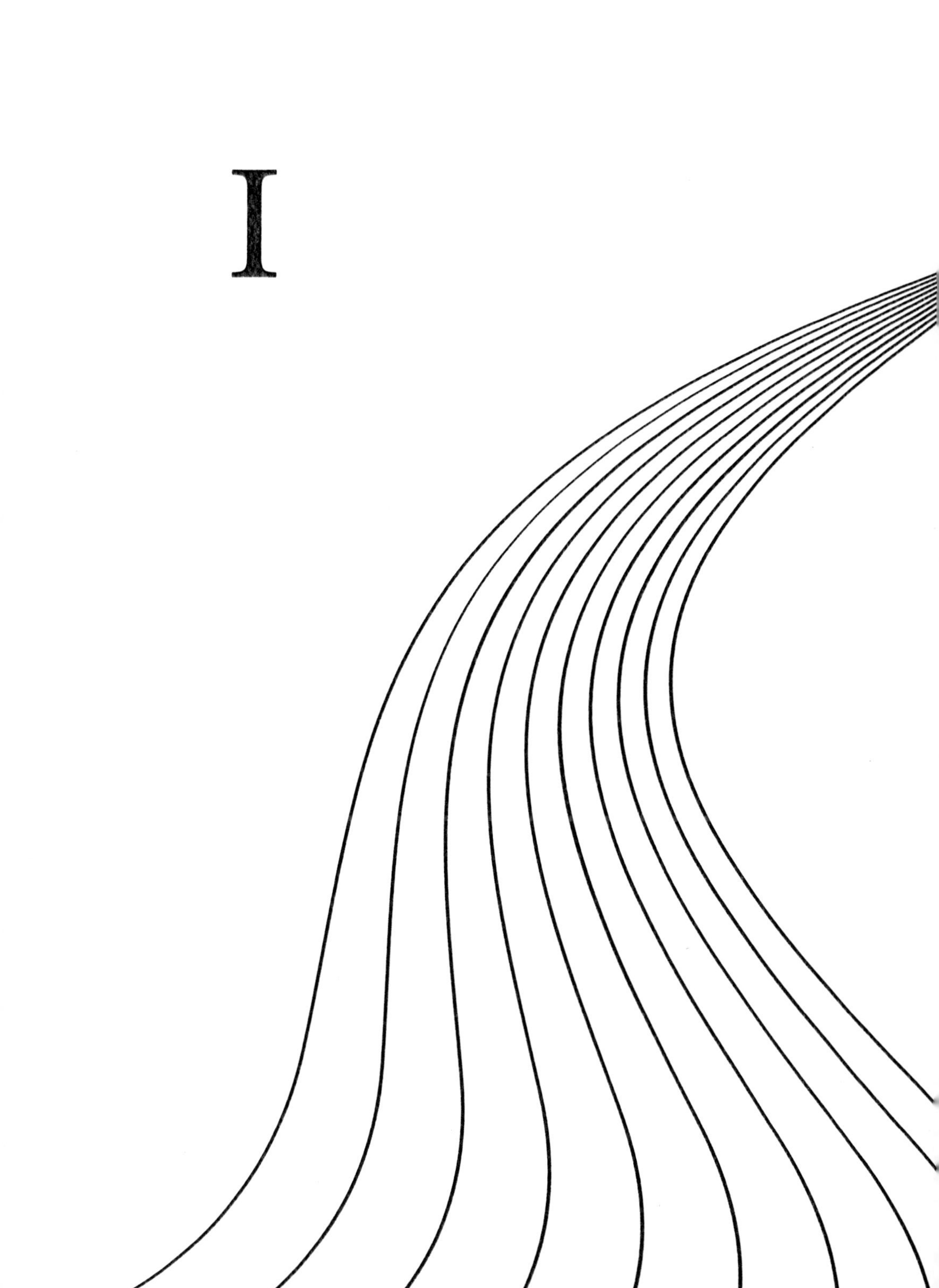

Night Ships at the Port

I whose feet
in a contact zone

among lives
that will one day

fit in a jar
ferried breath

free from wells
& coral skies

What cargo
do I carry

What weapons
have I held

Gising

I can't remember
if it was barbed wire

or bits of beerglass
the bougainvillea towered over,

or an orange boomerang
then a scar under my eye.

One day, I want to retire
from seeing only spectacle.

Live long enough
to grow with my hands.

Press one's fingers into the dirt.
Gather beans. Make of it a warm bowl.

Feed my child.
Muscle a cramped road.

This is my signal. Today, I will celebrate.
Here is a grandfather

in a bucket hat,
bobbing to "Purple Rain."

Sunflowers from Sxótsaqel
spring out of his car window.

A Basset Hound says hello.
Earlier, my nephew had a thread

around his two milk teeth.
His mother by the door.

I wish you were there to see him.
The way he said *Wow*.

In our language, to wake up
rhymes with blessing.

The sun is
beginning to line my irises.

My niece, how she sings
"Baby Shark."

What else can I tell you?
Let us go.

There is side-street parking.
The ticket machine

looks like a pair of binoculars
across an orchid mural.

Keys & raincoat are on the table.
I have been late all this time.

Kundiman

Not far into the end
    of the trail, a snake
leaves its old dress
    & I recall the house.
The one whose door
    you knocked on,
its brushed nickel cold.
    There was light on the porch
but no one came out.
    Not even eyes or a slight
shuffle from the curtains.
    Asking you to leave.
At night, your name
    in the sky and once
on the small of my back.
    If the slither of loss
is within earshot,
    I was told to look up.
But I think. Wait.
    Recall hissing
& what might hiss again.
    This house,
a house blown open.

Girl on Fire

There is no thermometer for mania   yet I felt feverish
Everything glowed
Nothing had a shadow   What faced me I touched   like honeyed gold
melting on my hands & I could not keep up   all this dripping   on the ground
Wearing a wetsuit from Valhalla   I spilled and spun   in the underpass of
                    skytrains
until I tripped on concrete   islands of bruises forming on both my shins   silver coins
I spent & overspent beyond   my means, myself   an ambulance blaring
into the Emergency Room   winter tires both cold and warm   in January rain

The Country I Come From is Called The Temp Agency of The Planet

To the man
at Tim Horton's
who shouted, "Come on,
where my Filipinos at?"
I wish I was a whip
speaker.
Instead of freezing
in front of coffee beans.
It's all good, just
insert your debit card.
Thousands of timbits
in a briefcase
I hauled home as if
I have no history.
Diabetes both sides
of my kin,
red dots on a map
scattering.
I thought poems,
should they earn
enough punchlines –
as stellar scorecard of words –
could offer a way out.
But I wake up
in the break room,
embarrassed.
I drooled again,
this poem is only a poem
and it is for the shoulders.

Pre-existing Conditions

When the teacher said the tragic
& the comic are parts of the same whole,

I laughed.

More than five hundred years ago,
Spain & Portugal divided the world in half.

As per creative advice, this needed
embellishment.

More than five hundred years ago,
Spain & Portugal divided the world in half
so it was not uncommon to hear I own half of you.

(I am laughing so I won't cry.)

Like a headstrong historian, I wanted to probe
what centuries of being owned
catapults into a psyche

but residing in Vancouver and spending time
as a function of money,

just plug in entities to replace Spain and Portugal
for the moment & most likely, the hustle leaves
you a husk.

Facing the bathroom mirror, say *Subservience*,
a pill on the counter you swallow before daybreak

subservience, subservience,
subservience, subservience,
until you arrive at subversive

over and over across Mountain View
Cemetery, over and over on Marpole,

Propped up on La-Z-boy &
gazing at Monterona's paintings

in the basement of a greying house
on a plot that refused to be sold,

I dreamt of coconuts –

        smashed

and smashing on the ground.

Duplex Ukol Sa Utang Na Loob

I was scared my anger meant I was unlovable.
Anger, I had nowhere to put this down.

Anger, where do I put you down?
The Tagalog word for pomegranate is Granada.

Having eaten what I can't detonate, I agonize.
I agonize over gut flora while taking photographs.

I take photographs of pine, plum, & magnolia.
The trees detonate pine, plum, & magnolia.

Without a camera, my cousin saw a child explode.
I was a child of explosion after explosion.

What does it mean to witness an explosion? Carry it home?
My roots, their ears were once children too.

Anger, I look at the water in your eyes.
I was scared my anger meant I was unlovable.

Flickering

I have an uncle whose name always comes up
 every time I am asked about my family's medical history.

In the story my father tells me, my uncle would bolt
 out of bed after midnight and whisper to his siblings,

"I have the perfect plan on how to get to the moon."
 On the morning that followed, he landed his fist

on their neighbour's cheek in a parking lot where
 young brown boys brandished their Bruce Lee moves.

There in the Devil's Island as he & his friends
 called it, he sustained an orbital fracture.

Sometimes I picture this uncle alive.
 Apparitions felt more than facts.

He'd gorge on bellies of milkfish after a day of waiting.
 Casting his lightweight rod into the sea.

I picture him close to the vast phosphoresence,
 One eye closed, the other squinting.

Impatient with the telescope yet eager to point
 to the Big Dipper, Orion, Cassiopeia.

With tattered medical records peeking out of his bag,
 we'd trade stories about the ward and drape them

around our shoulders like a prayer. We would move on.
 Ease touch where panic lives under the night sky.

With a swig of San Miguel, we'd talk about punches
 thrown during Thrilla in Manila and for the thousandth

time after the most heated argument with the rest of the clan,
 we'd resolve that Muhammad Ali is pound-for-pound the greatest

& in the quiet thereafter, there is breath.
 In the cadence of Ilonggo that raised me since childhood,

he would say just because our brains were on fire,
 does not mean we were only made to burn things down.

As we throw more wood into the heating pile, I hyperfocus
 on the silvery tips of his moustache to distract myself

from the heave of my chest, children of regrets
 & what we believe we have torched with our words.

From the shoreline, we'd recount what we love.
 Here is some honey for the wound. Here are your butterflies.

Kokomban

In the cat fur back seat of my parents' pick-up truck
    I spot the word & howl. Kokomban!

Summer beams through the glass window
    warming calves I slap while laughter spills

like a slurpee onto a friend who's just come back.
    Kokomban like bread rolls with coconut jam.

Someone's kid sprints with bagfuls
    past the basketball court & the prime hour

of playing. Kokomban unbroken silver hair
    your brother plucks out of your bedhead

they tuck in their jeans as they walk away
    & warn this is all it takes to make another you.

Kokomban a ban on breakfast cereals
    until unions of farmers & factory workers are paid.

Organizers who hurry for birthdays,
    beat the traffic instead of getting shot.

Kokomban, I take off my cap.
    The gap between what I heard & what I read

closed for a second. This kind of paper
    named after "coupon" & "bond."

Sold at the sari-sari store, piece by piece.
    Couponbond, Coponband, Kokomban.

Water

Before you could talk, you swam,
took up residence
in water

To decipher if there is life out there
the first thing
astronauts look for is water

It seems in order
to live a river of stars
we trade for a roadhouse of startles

What is it
The hush that hardens you and me
over time

Hear water gushing
over a grandfather's
scraped knee

Hear water like hunger
lacing its shoes, rallying
on a bright spit-laden street

“Why don’t you just take your meds?”

Of course
I chose
the brain
a grandmother
to hold
by the arm
at night
as she goes
to bed,
right hand
on her belly.
that must
rise & fall.
Snoring even.
Former gust
of wind
on my eyelash.
(Who watched
me grow.)
Once
outside
her house
by the streetlamp
a dog
on my left
barked so loud
I swerved
& bumped
my leg
into a fire
hydrant.
I ran
my hand
over my leg
& the bruise

that was
& briefly checked
my hip
(the good one)
when the doctor
at Crosstown
warned (the switch
from) Quetiapine
to Lithium
will, from the gut
& heart,
relay the risk
(of damage)
to the thyroid
and kidneys.

Copernicus

The sun reports
for work

I head home

The sun reports
for work

I plop in bed

Overcast
with the assist

Pillow supports
my neck

I locate my axes

Violences

When the conversation turns & the driver extols endurance,
sainthood at all costs, the jacaranda blooms
a persimmon hue I crane my neck for,
quiet orange leaves, flock of firebirds in the freeway.
Elbow on armrest as tripod, I shoot & I shoot.
Pretend to marvel for the rest of the ride.

Walking Home

Between marigolds
& gladiolas

on my way
to the neighbour's

fig tree
first day

solo renter
what is buried

beneath my chest
finds its way

to my roof,
the roof

of one's mouth.
Perfect punitive.

Duffel bag
of winnings.

One *should*
after the other

softening
underfoot.

Third Person Singular

What if hysterical
had historical roots

What if roots were
an unrestrained show of colour

What if we kept
writing about violets

If we can't (yet)
about the violence

What if we removed
the knife

What if we stopped
the blow

II

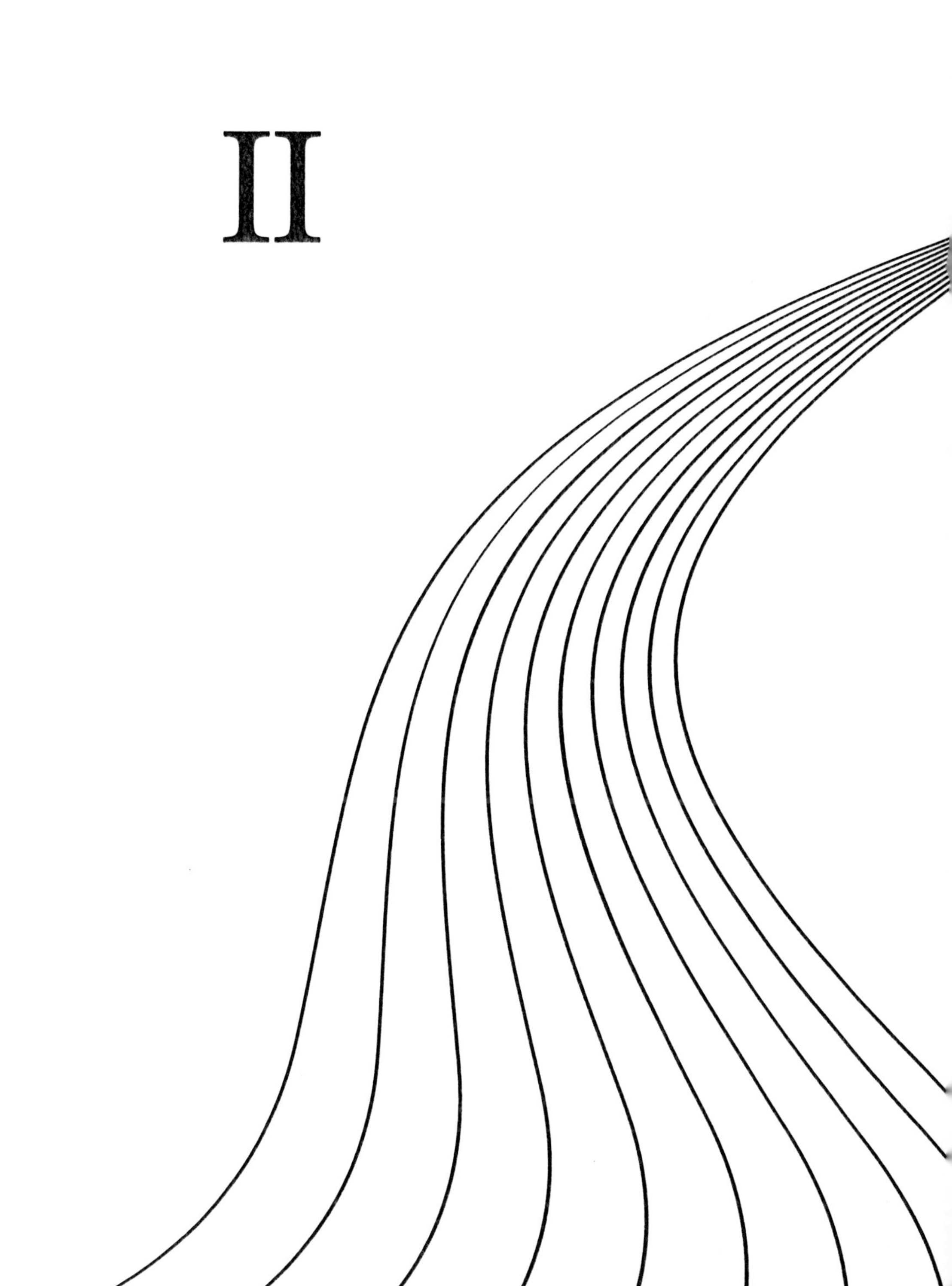

For Us

For us who think in constellation
instead of consequence.

Open –
a word we fear
for what swerves.

What fills.

Once, in a psych ward,
I traced small dents on the wall

as if each showed the earth
from a single cell to a dying beloved.

We root as much as we can and yet.

Elegy from a Wave

I do not know what it is like
to lose a beloved to the sea.

Their body found
by watchful eyes

of a fisherman's tugboat.
The raft it tows

so close to one's leaving.
Dark moon of the body

kissed by salmon & krill
tearing across the water

before the blaze of a copper sky.
I do not know what it is like

to line the shore with flowers.
To surround their grave

with bloom & cake
on the eve of their birthday.

In light of this
shortness of breath, I remember

those who speak to them at night,
who call their names

with their dreams & hands
& sleeping mouths.

Limits

I don't detest the lightning
        on tracks, but horses

& horses within them
        are on their own.

In the race, they go
        & go like dentures

to a foodie. Fractures,
        in part, pay

for the feast & fireworks.
        At night they plunge.

No foul questions.
        Hurt or hunger.

Streaks in the sky
        without being a tree.

Wreck

For Aylan Kurdi

That sand can be cot
a child's cheek

cold on the shore
& the curving tide

Inhaling   Exhaling
for two

His shirt dyed red
(Mystery Space Riders)

In the dream
felled log houses

The longest river
not a river

Accents

I had a pendant
        slashed
from a braided
        olive cord
I tucked
        inside
a lacquered
        music box
with a pearl
         earring
I bought
        from a kiosk
in Divisoria.
        Plaster of Paris
in need of repair
        a small girl
with green sitar
        seated close
to what forms
        when irritants
cloister
        around an oyster
in its shell.
        Faraway
from waters
        soothing
I wonder
        about
this kind of sitting
        & what happens
might I
        could I
whole body
        the ocean's
dirt & debris.

At this point
I would like to say
for many
my father
talks funny.
For me
he sings
as if his words
are waves
lulling the stern
of a blue boat
back to shore
ili-ili tulog anay
ili-ili tulog anay.

English Lessons in a Former Colony

Not cathedrals
or knuckles
outside its steel gates.

Not palms rushed
by need or else
pressed upwards

covering their children
with prayers
before the tricycles

& roosters.
Not classroom
letters as the law

& license plates
to shiny futures.
Not the Mayor

in pineapple fiber
silver bulletproof
cruising,

"Do you know
who I am?"
or the robber

he ordered
to eat the stacks
of bills he stole,

not tetanus
straight into
the stomach.

Not the hand shy
& forgoing
what it thinks

in fear of how
it sounds.
Not nuns,

centipedes
or gym teachers
who move you.

Not *is* or *are*
drilled on blue red blue
until the chalk breaks

into a screech,
& elders tug
our ankles cold.

Not the whiz
of metal trays.
Furious spoons

& forks at lunch.
Not a hint
of cockroach on rice.

Not wrists
on desks like onions
on a chopping board.

Listens,
believing
it's all in the mind.

1996

In the living room couch tinged with Tiger Balm we spotted
two raccoons scurrying into the brambled curve Damp tails

escaping rubbish from the neighbour's fence We cheered them on

appeardisappear a memory of freshly picked forepaws

darting sampaguita into the rims of armalites & green tanks

bullets the first- second- third- & fourth quarter storms

Torn muscle ache of the bone one sear suture
not enough to topple or camouflage tyrannical heads of state

in my brain I have one misfiring mistrusting mom
on my corner of the bed when she pulled my sleeping feet

held my cracked heels The largest tub of petroleum jelly
leaning against her hip perfect grease for a solid axe kick

Flight

After Ross Gay

The start
of the move

was slow
& furious

planting
the ball

of the foot
against 4.5 billion

years of earth
before the body

like a flock of doves
rose towards

a windmill dunk
which misses

by the way,
but how

many times
have we

been launched
into the air

& upon landing
say to each other

what made
a handful

of gerberas blush —
this try

& try again
we believe in —

our sheepish grins
gassed up

Merienda

Under a guava tree
 on a green fishnet hammock
 my grandmother & I.

We shoo small
 bloodsuckers,
 thorax on our caramel cake.

Lola, it is June
 I am back to school
 lunch box & rain gear

ready with my name
 handwritten by you.
 Dengue too is becoming

a full-blown fiesta
 the funerals we visit
 generous with snacks.

This season's eggs
 cannot lay in water
 containers shut tight.

We know what to do
 when refined sugar starts
 to scratch our throats.

Inside her house
 we boil a kettle. Pour
 mugs of oregano.

Silver door swings open.
 We kill mosquitoes
 that remind us we are meat.

Dear Jolina

From the bench where I sit,
the sidewalk is livid.

Vendors erupt at rims
that step on the gas

& rush through flood.
No one wants to read

wet newspapers.
You can't use it to wrap

diesel-smoked cabbage
or string beans.

Customers can smell.
Pinch them. You're done.

My eyes are
on the butterfly clips.

Shiny even
when veiled with plastic.

They turn heads into pop
star real estate, glittery

wings yanked or borrowed
until owned.

Our styled locks,
in this instance,

not gardens,
but fight zones.

This filled me
with the passion

to commit.
My hands,

after a long day,
like stealthy guards

to my bulging navy
blue skirt.

Pockets
chrysalis-silent.

Language Arts

some mouths misread *mouths* for *milk*
they are mouths to feed they are faces to love

Bahay-bata

There is a hole
in a honey cruller

a two-year-old's
half-open hand

can fit right into.
Snug on the wrist.

Licking
their first bangle.

In my dream
at the park

they pick up a flute
on their way

to the trampoline.
They jump

gums bleed
& I scramble

for an ice cube
to place on their tongue.

Maybe this is not
mine to feel

but I do.
Even on days

clear of clouds
folded & soft

like a family of pajamas
moonwalking

chamomile years
the hole reasserts

itself as a crater.
When I dare,

I ask it
to bless me.

I wear my best
lilac shirt

like party
streamers.

Writer's Archive

After Joanne Arnott

I placed years of words inside a word cloud
as an attempt to sift through
a record of thoughts racing
I prefer as rain on my rubber boots,
small & wet I can shake off by the door
beside a mop & a red bucket.
The words in large serif
constellate on the screen: woman, want,
trees, arms, home, called, look, enough.
You may lose face, but what happens
grows in you & gives you a vision.
This morning shade once auburn has now
marooned. A cul-de-sac to park sunsets.
Woman. Want. Trees. Arms. Home. Called.
Look. Enough. Each full stop unspooling
the Cardinal & Bluebird privacy of things.

Prayer at Grad Party

The DJ plays
Carly Rae's "Cut to the Feeling"
near the washroom & we split
the last banana-cue.
Drink from the same solo cup.
As we stare at the neon dance floor,
glow sticks on our wrists,
her pinky inches closer to mine
& the track spinning on my mind
switches to The Cranberries' "Linger"
before the meme "You must leave
room for the Holy Spirit" leads me
to desperate waters. Dear Jesus,
I don't want you to forgive me.
I am so with you loving
God's children. Please come
see me & her & how we eat.
The music we are.
Red & full of ceiling.

Chicharon From Kay Market

There is a heartache
I prefer to eat

with iced-cold pop.
Pork rinds

steeped
in bubbling oil,

crispy fried,
lightweight,

it smacks me in the face.

Reader, my mother
tells me

"Its crunching sound
is as satisfying as it tastes."

Church of salt & fat
on the lips that fall

on my shirt & sweatpants.
It floors me

how chicharon crumbs
are never crumbs.

Bulaklak, bituka,
laman served

with spicy vinegar
& just like that

the whole bag crackles
& bows.

Real Talk

Dear Jesus, I am ticked off
by the passage where you suffer
for my transgressions.
First of all, they are mine.
Even soggy mulch in the gutter
once shimmered gold.
I can get behind the cross
& crown of thorns but what moved
me the most was when you picked
the fallen ear on the ground
and put it back on to the soldier
about to arrest you.
In the book of John
you said there is no greater love
than for a man to lay down
his life for his friend.
Did you ever have to hide
your feelings for John?
Why must love be premised
on self-annihilation?
I was flustered when you replied,
"It's okay, Girl. I'll live."

Islands Along Mount Pleasant

Pockets out of quarters
    past Pedal Heads
& a row of daffodils,
    you misheard *flawed*
as *flowered* and filled
    what was missing
in the air with *Yes*
    everywhere people flower.
We left an archipelago
    whose elders weather
heart attack & heat stroke
    as if illness
were a cluster of islands
    we cross
so it crosses back.
    Today is the fourth
day of spring
    & we live
in a city that unroofs
as often as it rains.
    Under a glass awning,
we trace patterns
    on our palms.

Cruel Strokes

When I found out that my tongue

could be a scythe
on a shearing spree

I decided I would only eat
what would make my mouth bloom.

Later on I learned
that to speak only in flowers

in a field like this
is the sharpest blade of all.

Child

Child whose worry is mercury in the water, red marking the tide.
Child whose skin takes on the taste of the water they swim in.
Child whose eyes a quiet stream by the coffin.
Child whose eyes harden. Child whose eyes soften.
Child whose backpack swells with quail eggs & sampaguita to sell
by the roadside.
Child whose arms a heavy nest & to the green she waters she
screams
"Mabuhay! Mabuhay!"
Child whose mothers feed the faces she loves by working overseas.
Child whose daughters' scent visits them in their dreams.
Child whose shoes work hard to remember. Child whose shoes
work hard to forget.
Child whose laugh can tank a ship. Child whose heart is a fish that
slips.

Acknowledgements

Shane Neilson who saw several iterations of the poems & edited with expansive care

Jeremy Luke Hill & Gordon Hill Press for developing *From The Shoreline* into a whole book

Karla Comanda, Marc Perez, Chris Nazaire, Hessed Torres, Jeremiah Carag, Lydia Du Bois, Johna Baylon, Phebe Ferrer, Alyssa Sy de Jesus, Teilhard Paradela, Dennis Gupa, Chaya Ocampo Go, Charis Tolentino, Erie Maestro, Elizabeth Armerding, Barbara Carter, Yong Nan Kim, Zofia Rose Musiej, Deborah Vieyra, Martha Warren, Jacqui Wilcocks, Catherine Yeung, Jane Shi, Ahmed Said, Alex Watson, Chelsea Williams, DeShara Suggs-Joe, Hayley Mojica, Julian Guy, Lana Marilyn, Maryam Gunja, Renee Kay, Sarah Blumenthal, Siri Helleloid, Evelyn Lau, Fiona Lam, Renee Saklikar, Shira Erlichman for their presence in the world & the art they make

Oliver de la Paz for his guidance and mentorship

Selina Boan for her editorial gifts that shaped many of the poems in this book

Jonina Kirton for her kind & generous seeing I can't forget

Angel Nafis for her incredible support, how she gives to her students, lifts their languages & spirits up

Joanne Arnott for what the song is about, opening the door towards all that is good, & truly for everything

SFU Writer's Studio, Andrew Chesham, Laura Farina, Kiran Dhanoa, a community for emerging writers I'm grateful to have been a part of

Rahila's Ghost Press & Frog Hollow Press for their encouragement & for publishing versionsof these poems in chapbook form

Friends & family especially Al, maraming salamat

About the Author

Steffi Tad-y is a poet & writer from Manila. She currently lives in Vancouver located in the territories of the Musqueam, Squamish, & Tsleil-Waututh Nations.